THE NO-NONSENSE KEY

Read *How to Choose a Lawyer*

- If you have a specific legal problem
- If you think that you might have a legal problem and want to know where to get the best advice
- If you are in business for yourself or are thinking of starting your own business
- If you have been injured, either financially or physically, and want to protect your legal rights

NO-NONSENSE FINANCIAL GUIDES:

How to Finance Your Child's College Education
How to Use Credit and Credit Cards
Understanding Treasury Bills and Other U.S. Government Securities
Understanding Tax-Exempt Bonds
Understanding Money Market Funds
Understanding Mutual Funds
Understanding IRAs
Understanding Common Stocks
Understanding the Stock Market
Understanding Stock Options and Futures Markets
How to Choose a Discount Stockbroker
How to Make Personal Financial Planning Work for You
How to Plan and Invest for Your Retirement
Understanding Estate Planning and Wills
The New Tax Law and What It Means to You

NO-NONSENSE REAL ESTATE GUIDES:

Understanding Condominiums and Co-ops
Understanding Buying and Selling a House
Understanding Mortgages
Refinancing Your Mortgage

HOW TO CHOOSE A LAWYER

Phyllis C. Kaufman
& Arnold Corrigan

LONGMEADOW PRESS

How to Choose a Lawyer

Cover art © 1986 by Longmeadow Press.
Design by Adrian Taylor. Production services by William S. Konecky Associates, New York.

ISBN 0-681-40146-X

Printed in the United States of America

0 9 8 7 6 5 4 3 2

In loving memory of my wonderful mother,
Gertrude Friend Kaufman

Acknowledgements

The authors wish to thank Martin Heller, Esquire; M. Shirley Young, Esquire; Jules I. Whitman, Esquire; Allen B. Dubroff, Esquire; Steven I. Weisburd, Esquire; and Jacqueline Levitt Laskoff for sharing their knowledge and expertise in the preparation of this book.

TABLE OF CONTENTS

PART I—WHEN DO YOU NEED A LAWYER?

1

INTRODUCTION

When do you need a lawyer? More often than you may think. Of course, there are obvious situations where a lawyer is essential—if you have been sued or if you have been accused of a crime. But there are many other situations where a lawyer can help you cure a present problem or help you take actions to prevent a problem from arising in the future.

Life has become so complex that virtually everyone needs to consult with a lawyer at some time. In short, a well-chosen lawyer can be one of your greatest assets— helping to protect your rights, serving as a financial and business advisor, or acting as your confidant.

So it's not only people in trouble who need a lawyer—it's anyone with a family or involved in business or complicated dealings with others. The real problem is finding the right lawyer to hire and for the right price. That's what *How to Choose a Lawyer* is about.

2

PREVENTIVE LAWYERING

When you engage the services of an attorney is almost as important as which attorney you select. One serious mistake is waiting too long before seeking professional help. Chapters 3 to 6 are intended to make you more alert to the circumstances when a lawyer's help is advisable.

As we said earlier, it's easy to know that you need a lawyer when you suddenly find yourself in the middle of a lawsuit or accused of a crime. It's harder to know when to go to a lawyer to *avoid* problems. Contrary to popular belief, lawyers are trained to prevent problems, not to cause them. And using a lawyer *before* trouble arises can often save you time, aggravation, and money. So preventive lawyering, like preventive medicine, can be a lifesaver.

In business, preventive lawyering can insure clarity in contracts, negotiations, or business dealings. By eliminating misunderstandings and confusion, you can often avoid costly litigation and other problems in the future.

In personal situations, preventive lawyering can also save you time, money, and distress. For example, if you are buying a new home on which work remains to be done, a lawyer can protect your rights in case of poor performance by the builder. Or, if you want to make sure that your children are protected in case of your disability, a lawyer can write a trust document for their benefit.

An Ounce of Prevention

Most of us are at least a little bit lazy about taking action now to prevent future problems. And many people hesitate to pay a lawyer's fee until it has become absolutely necessary. But the old adage, "An ounce of prevention is worth a pound of cure," still holds true. Usually the best way to improve your future is to invest a little time, effort, and money right now.

3

PERSONAL AND FAMILY MATTERS

It used to be assumed that only the very rich needed a lawyer to assist with their personal and family affairs. That is no longer true, and in the 1980s, virtually everyone will need to consult with a lawyer at some time, even if it is only to write a simple will.

Your Legal Check-Up

The first question many people ask is, "Should I have a family lawyer, just as I have a family doctor?" The answer is probably "Yes." Like a good family doctor, a lawyer you trust and can consult before problems arise is a source of comfort and security. Of course, the more complicated your legal situation is, the more you may require legal advice on a regular basis. But always knowing that you have a lawyer who understands your personal affairs, is familiar with your family, and has an objective understanding of your situation, is a comforting necessity in today's complex world.

Ordinarily you should not need a yearly personal legal check-up in the way that you should have a yearly physical exam. But going over your affairs, updating your will, insurance, contractual and tax obligations, and other matters every few years with a competent attorney in whom you have confidence is an excellent idea that could save you time, money, and heartache in the future. If you can build a long-term relationship with a "family lawyer" you trust, this kind of periodic review will come naturally and will relieve your life of considerable areas of problems and worry.

Your Will

A will is a document that tells the world what to do with your money, personal belongings, and property after you die. Making a will is essential if you have anything to leave and you want to make sure that it goes to the person(s) you select. A will is also essential if you want to make sure that your children are cared for. If you die "intestate"—that is, without a will—your wealth will be distributed according to the intestacy laws of your state, without regard to your wishes and often in ways completely different from what you would have intended.

It is possible for you to handwrite a will, giving directions for the disposition of your property and avoiding the use of a lawyer. This is a risky business. Some states do not recognize handwritten (called "holographic") wills, while other states place many technical requirements on them, such as witnesses, use of certain "operative words," notarization, etc. The inadvertent omission of even one of these requirements can invalidate a document that you have carefully thought out and executed.

Wills should be revised and rethought every few years, or whenever your circumstances change. For these reasons, and because of the tax and other requirements that exist, a will and its revisions have become one of the primary reasons to seek legal advice for many Americans. Any attorney who functions as a family lawyer is assumed and expected to have some knowledge of wills. In addition, a legal specialty in wills and estate planning has evolved.

Children

Caring for your children, in case you die or become incapacitated, is another important reason to seek a lawyer's help. You might want to set up trust funds for your children or to appoint a guardian to care for them. Or, you might have a child with a physical or mental handicap who requires special consideration. You might want to ensure that all of your children will have money set aside to attend college or will receive an income for a certain period. All these things can be accomplished by a lawyer specializing in trusts and estates.

Adopting a child is a matter that requires expert legal advice to ensure the security of your new family. There are attorneys who specialize in this type of family law.

Marriage and Living Together

Normally, you think of hiring a lawyer when you intend to get a divorce. But today, many people are using lawyers to set up certain financial arrangements *before* marriage—partly to avoid disputes during the marriage, partly to prevent and anticipate certain problems if the marriage should end in divorce.

Prenuptial (also called antenuptial) agreements are becoming commonplace. These agreements, drawn with the aid of lawyers representing both parties, determine the rights of each party in case of divorce or death of one spouse. Money, property, and even child custody and support matters are settled and agreed upon before the problems arise, allowing both parties to enter the marriage knowing what their rights will be should it fail.

A properly drawn prenuptial agreement is a valid and binding legal contract. Courts are reluctant to overturn any properly executed contract, and a court will usually uphold the validity of a prenuptial agreement unless it is determined that one party did not fully and completely disclose all assets prior to the signing of the agreement, or, in some states, if each party was not represented by a lawyer.

The concept of prenuptial agreements has recently expanded, and many unmarried couples who decide to live together now elect to enter into this type of agreement. Some extend the terms to cover their eventual marriage, divorce, or death.

All this may sound mercenary and antithetical to the true purpose of marriage, and perhaps it is. But in today's litigious society, where divorce is commonplace and marriage not necessarily a lifelong commitment, it is realistic to enter into a marriage knowing what your rights will be if it should terminate.

Divorce

In a divorce, the primary issue usually turns out to be who gets what, when, and for how long. The economic issues involved in terminating a marriage usually take center stage, even ahead of the emotional issues.

There are very few cases when a lawyer is not needed to aid each party in a divorce. Even in a "no-fault" state (that is, a state where divorce can be obtained by mutual consent rather than by the allegation of wrongdoing), when the divorce is totally amicable and there are no children or property involved, it is still probably a good idea for each party to have the documents reviewed by an attorney to make sure that the details have been handled properly and that no one's rights have been neglected.

If you do have a totally amicable divorce, in a no-fault state, with no children and an agreed-upon division of marital assets, this could be the right situation to use one of the less-costly "storefront" law firms that we will discuss in Chapter 13.

However, if the divorce is not agreed on by both parties, or if there are custody or property questions to resolve, then a specialist in marital matters should be consulted. Divorce is a specialty full of technicalities that, in a complicated, or emotional situation, should be handled by someone with expertise in the area.

4

BUSINESS AND REAL ESTATE

Starting or running a business and buying or selling real estate are prime reasons for seeking legal advice. Let's start with your business.

Starting a Business

No matter how small your business is at the beginning, an attorney can be of great help. The form of your business is an important legal matter. You need to know the various ramifications of operating as a corporation, partnership, or sole proprietorship. If you want to start small, a proprietorship may be ideal. But you must understand when to adopt the corporate form (a move which will limit your liability in case of problems), and how to make basic tax decisions. Your lawyer will also work with your accountant in preparing your tax returns.

The second important legal area is the protection of your rights and business assets. For example, you might be selling a product that should be protected by a patent, or your business name and logo might be so unique that they should be trademarked. Finally, if there is written matter involved in your sales brochures or other material, a lawyer will tell you whether it ought to be copyrighted.

Employees and their rights and your obligations are other areas where a lawyer's help is essential. You will need to know about pensions, health benefits, and other duties of an employer. You may also need a lawyer's help in drafting employment contracts and negotiating terms and conditions.

Buying a Business

When you buy a business, a lawyer should look over all the documents, and perhaps negotiate the purchase with or for you. There are many details to be settled when purchasing an ongoing business, and each one is too complicated to accomplish without expert assistance. These include appraising the value of the assets, attaching a value to goodwill and other intangibles, setting the terms of payment, figuring the tax ramifications of the purchase, determining continuing obligations to the seller and the consequences of potential business failure, and assigning rights to the property purchased. Each detail must be spelled out correctly if you are to be protected.

A lawyer who specializes in business and tax matters can be especially helpful in this area.

Selling a Business

The same advice is true if you are the seller of a business. In addition to selling the machines, property, and other tangible assets, you may also be selling intangibles such as goodwill or the use of your name.

A competent professional will protect your rights and help structure the most favorable deal. Among other matters, you need to be sure that payment will be made to you as agreed and that the payment arrangements are as favorable as possible from a tax point of view.

Business Matters

A lawyer can be your most valued friend and confidant regarding your business affairs. Beginning with the formation of your business and the choice of its legal form (corporation, sole proprietorship, or partnership) and going on to its tax structure and even of the purchase of equipment and the sale of goods or services, a good business attorney is essential. If you have employees, you may need the advice of both an attorney and an accountant to make sure you are complying with the tax and labor laws. A lawyer who serves many businesses will often be able to give you valuable advice going beyond the strictly legal area.

Employment Contracts

Negotiating an employment contract for yourself can be tricky, and you may want to seek the advice of an attorney to guide you through the process. If you are in this type of situation, you undoubtedly know that salary isn't the only type of compensation you can receive. There are retirement plan and severance pay provisions as well as "perks" such as an automobile or an automobile allowance, for which you will want to negotiate. A good attorney will be able to help you negotiate more effectively, and an employer who really wants your services should not be offended or fail to hire you because you have obtained legal advice. If the employer is offended, you should perhaps think twice about taking the job. If they don't want you to understand and assert your rights before you begin work, they will perhaps not honor your rights later on if problems arise.

Being Fired

The law regarding an employee who has been fired from a job, whether or not the employee has a contract, has been expanding. A doctrine of "at will" employment has arisen recently, granting to employees who work without the benefit of a contract certain rights upon firing. If you are fired, a plaintiff's injury lawyer or labor lawyer can advise you of your rights and may possibly be of great assistance

Real Estate

Buying or selling real estate is an area where legal problems often arise.

In many cases, the transaction is uncomplicated and the services of a lawyer aren't really required. When problems develop, however, a lawyer can be a

lifesaver. Hiring a lawyer early in the real estate transaction to write and negotiate agreements of sale, hold
escrow payments, see to the details of the transaction,
and be available to "trouble shoot" in case problems
arise, is a wise piece of insurance which will cost you
very little compared to the amount you are spending
on the purchase or receiving from the sale. The lawyer
you engage should be someone experienced in real estate transactions.

Buying A Home

There are many details, potential problems, and pit-
falls that can plague you when purchasing a home—
whether it is a house, condominium, or cooperative.

Once you have found the home you want, you will
make an "offer" for the house, backed by a "good
faith" deposit. An agreement of sale is then written.
The agreement of sale binds the buyer to purchase and
the seller to sell the property on a definite date, for a
specified amount of money, and under certain terms
and conditions.

A good real estate attorney will ensure that each
word in the agreement reflects your best interest. For
example, if the property is new, the agreement can protect you in case all the work is not completed by the
settlement date. If you are having alterations or special
details added to your property, an attorney will
include each item to be changed or added in the agreement of sale. If you are purchasing an existing property, you want to ensure that your rights to professional inspection, termite certification, good title, etc.,
are protected and that otherwise the agreement will be
cancelled and your deposit returned. In addition, if you
want the chandelier in the living room and the book-
cases in the den, an attorney will include these items.

Other more technical items, such as mortgage contingency, zoning, escrow, and risk of loss clauses will
also be written by your lawyer. The real estate agent
through whom you purchased the home may tell you
that he/she will write the agreement of sale for you and
that you need not spend additional money hiring a

13

lawyer. Be careful. Remember that the real estate agent works for and is paid by the seller. You should have someone who works for you negotiating on your behalf.

Selling a Home

When you are the seller, you want a lawyer to make sure that you will get your money on the date specified and that you will be entitled to damages if the buyer decides to cancel. You want an airtight contract in any case, ensuring that you receive the sales proceeds when and as agreed upon, but this will be particularly critical if you are buying another home and timing the sale to coincide with your purchase. An attorney with real estate expertise can often save you money as well as trouble and anxiety.

A Basic Rule

Whether in business, real estate, or any other area, let us emphasize one basic rule: engage an attorney and let him/her help you *before* you sign any documents. Afterwards may be too late. If you say, "I want to show this to my lawyer before I sign it," and the other party objects, you have reason to be doubly cautious. As we said earlier, "An ounce of prevention. . . ."

5

ACCIDENTS AND INJURIES

The area of accidents and injuries is a specialized area in the law known as "torts." A tort is a non-contractual civil wrong or injury.

Crimes are a criminal matter, tried in the criminal courts. Torts are civil matters, tried in the civil courts. Punishment for a crime is determined under the criminal laws of a state and may involve jail and/or the payment of a fine to the state. Restitution to the person injured may or may not be included. The tort laws, on the other hand, allow recovery by the person injured for damage done, for example, to his/her body (including pain and suffering), property, and/or reputation.

If you have been the victim of a tort, you should generally use a lawyer to handle your case. In some jurisdictions, you may proceed for small amounts of monetary damages on your own (see Chapter 10). In the great majority of cases, however, a lawyer will ensure you a better recovery and fuller protection of your rights.

Accidents

Probably the most common tort is an automobile accident. If someone rear-ends your car and you suffer whiplash, that is a tort and you may be able to sue and recover against the other driver (which, in practice, usually means against the other driver's insurance company).

If you drink a bottle of soda and accidentally swallow a foreign substance that somehow got into the soda during the bottling process, and that foreign substance makes you ill or causes other damage, you may decide to sue the beverage maker for the tort which has been committed against you.

  If you use a food processor and it blows up in your face, causing you injury, you may sue the manufacturer of the machine, the store which sold it to you, the distributor, and perhaps others in the chain of distribution.

All the above are examples of possible tort suits. The only way to know absolutely if you have suffered a tort for which the recovery of damages is possible is to consult an attorney. Lawyers who specialize in this area of the law are called plaintiff's injury lawyers.

6

CRIMINAL AND SPECIAL CASES

If You Are Accused of a Crime

If you are accused of a crime, or if you think that you might be so accused, get a lawyer. Not only your money may be at stake if you are convicted, but your liberty as well. In this area, it is always best to seek the help of a criminal law specialist. A good criminal lawyer can make all the difference.

Grand Jury

A grand jury is a body of citizens who investigate matters to determine if crimes have been committed and/or who hear the evidence regarding people accused of crimes and return indictments against them.

If you have been subpoenaed to testify before a grand jury investigating a specific matter, you should consult with an attorney prior to your testimony, especially if you have reason to think that you may be a target of or otherwise involved in the matters under investigation. Depending on the state, your attorney may or may not be allowed in the grand jury room with you. In federal court, attorneys are not permitted in the jury room. However, if your lawyer cannot be in the room with you, he/she may wait just outside and be consulted whenever you wish.

Bankruptcy

If you have debts which get out of control and which you can't repay, you may eventually be faced with the prospect of bankruptcy. Bankruptcy is a specialized area of the law, filled with details and requiring skill and experience. In the early stages of debt problems, you may be able to get help from credit counselling services and other sources. (See the No-Nonsense Financial Guide, *How to Use Credit and Credit Cards*.) But if you have business or personal problems which seem seriously to threaten bankruptcy, by all means consult a specialized attorney as soon as possible.

Patent, Trademark, and Copyright

If you are in business with a distinctive product or marketing approach, you may need a lawyer in the patent, trademark, or copyright areas. Patent lawyers must have a technical background and must also pass an examination prior to being admitted to practice before the U.S. Patent Office. There is no such requirement for lawyers dealing with trademark and copyright matters, although the three specialties tend to practice together. In addition, many entertainment lawyers specialize in the latter two areas. See Chapter 11.

Class Actions

We have put class actions in this chapter for want of a better place to include them.

A class action is a lawsuit brought by one or a number of injured parties on behalf of all others who, it is believed, have been similarly injured. Class actions are not criminal matters, even though they often involve violations of the securities, real estate, product liability, or antitrust laws

Notice of possible membership in a class action is usually given by mail. The notice will direct you to reply within a given number of days stating whether or not you want to join the class. You should by all means join unless you have a specific reason not to (for example, if you have your own separate lawsuit against the defendant). There is no reason to hire an attorney of your own, since the class will be represented by lawyers who expect to be well compensated for their time and effort if the suit is successful.

In class actions, many an individual has ended up with a sizable recovery for no more effort than signing on the line and licking a postage stamp. One of the authors, an avid shopper, became a member of a famous class action regarding price-fixing among three prominent New York retailers. After signing on as a member of the class, the only other thing that had to be done was to return to the shops some three years later to spend the $395 recovery!

PART II—WHERE TO FIND A LAWYER—A SHOPPER'S GUIDE

7

PERSONAL RECOMMENDATION

The best way to find a lawyer is through the personal recommendation of someone you trust. That advice will be particularly valuable, of course, if the recommended lawyer was used for a problem similar to yours.

Who to Ask

Your friends, neighbors, and relatives are obvious sources of information. If you are hesitant about involving them in your personal affairs, you should consider asking your minister, priest, or rabbi. Clergy often are good judges of their congregants and may be able to match you with someone they trust and with whom you would work well.

Your co-workers may also be a good source of information, or your supervisor. Casual acquaintances should not be overlooked as sources. Don't hesitate to talk to anyone who has had similar problems in the past and has had the opportunity of using an attorney.

Of course, when obtaining a personal reference, you must be sure of its source. Only ask people you respect. The opinion of a close relative or dear friend who has little common sense has no value. If you admire the opinions of your boss, or even your boss's boss, don't hesitate to ask him/her for a reference. Even, if you are not personally acquainted, the fact that you respect the person's opinion enough to ask will be flattering and should ensure a considered response.

Personal Experience

Make sure that the person whose recommendation you seek has had personal experience with the attorney he/she recommends. You aren't asking about reputation—you need personal experience. As we said, the best recommendation is from someone who has had a good experience with an attorney in a similar matter.

For example, if your close friend, whose opinions you respect, was involved in a divorce and you are also getting a divorce, your friend's opinion about his/her lawyer (and the opposing lawyer) should be valuable. However, if your friend was involved in a divorce and you need an attorney to handle the purchase of a house, then the recommendation may not be relevant.

Professional References

A recommendation from a professional with expertise in the area of your case could prove very valuable. For example, if your problem is an injury resulting from an accident, you might consult your physician. Your accountant will no doubt know of a competent tax attorney. And, if you are contemplating marriage or divorce, marriage counsellors or family therapists would be a good source of lawyer referral.

Don't forget bank officers and/or the chief financial officer where you work. These professionals come in contact with lawyers every day and should be able to give you excellent leads.

If you belong to any church, civic, or labor organizations, the other members could be a source of information. Also, if there is a law school in your area, you might try to contact a professor who teaches courses in the area of your problem and ask for a recommendation.

Other Lawyers

Lawyers often refer clients to specialists for matters they do not regularly handle, especially in areas where specialized knowledge and experience are essential. These recommendations are valuable. If you have any doubts about the judgment or reliability of the recommending lawyer, ask for a selection of other attorneys to interview.

One Warning

When dealing with referrals from lawyers and even from some other professionals, you should be aware that a fee, called a "referral fee," may be paid to the referrer by the referred lawyer. The American Bar Association Code of Professional Responsibility, which has been adopted as law in many states, has specific rules regarding referral fees. The code states that such a fee may be paid only if the agreement for payment is in writing, signed by both lawyers, and disclosed to and acknowledged by the client.

Three Guidelines

In summary, keep these three guidelines in mind when soliciting a personal recommendation for an attorney:

1. Try, whenever possible, to obtain opinions from people whose values and character you trust and respect.
2. In asking for a referral, make clear that you are looking for an attorney who has handled a case or cases similar to yours.
3. Make sure that your reference speaks from personal experience and not only from reputation or hearsay.

8

BAR ASSOCIATIONS, COURTS, AND LEGAL PUBLICATIONS

Bar Associations

Most local and/or state bar associations have lawyer referral services to assist people in finding a lawyer to handle their case. Your state or local bar association will inform you of the availability of such a referral service in your area. The service may also be listed in the Yellow Pages at the beginning of the section on "Lawyers."

These services vary in the amount of assistance they offer. Ask the person you speak to at the bar association how the listed attorneys are screened for inclusion on the list. In some areas, lawyers do not need to have any minimum qualifications before they can become part of the service, and lawyers' names are given out in rotation. In other services, lawyers must have a certain amount of experience before they can become part of the service. In some services, lawyers are listed and assigned to cases according to declared areas of specialization. Even in this case, however, you must try to determine if the bar association has screened the listed attorneys for competence in their specialty, or if the list is compiled merely on the attorney's declaration of specialization.

Often the lawyer referral service will offer you more than a name. For example, in some cities the service allows you to consult for a half-hour or so with an interviewing attorney for a minimal fee (often as low as $25). This brief consultation lets the attorney evaluate your problem and decide whether or not you actually need a lawyer. Many times, it is determined that your problem can be handled by an administrative agency or some other nonlawyer facility. If it is determined that you do need a lawyer, the interviewing attorney will select a suitable one from an available list.

If the low-cost interview is not available in your area, the lawyer referral service may still be a financial help, since some services require the listed lawyers to accept a reduced fee for all cases obtained from the service.

Court Personnel

Court officers, stenographers, and other personnel work with attorneys every day and are keenly aware of their personalities and competence. You might try asking individuals who work in the judicial system for recommendations, making sure that they refer you to lawyers with expertise in the area of your concern. A useful technique is to ask each reference for several names, and then interview only those lawyers whose names appear on more than one list.

Legal Publications

Virtually every city has a legal publication which describes current litigation and recently decided cases. You might do well to check these publications to see which attorneys have been handling matters similar to yours. They will be available at your local library or at bar association headquarters.

Martindale-Hubble Law Directory

The *Martindale-Hubble Law Directory* has, for over 100 years, listed the education, affiliations, areas of expertise, and biographical data of members of the bar of the United States and Canada. This publication is available at your public library.

We don't suggest using *Martindale-Hubble* as your first source of information when choosing a lawyer. It doesn't really give you enough information about each lawyer's experience in order to make a selection; also, fees are not given.

But you may find *Martindale-Hubble* useful in certain respects. Let's say that you have been given a list of three names by your references. You might research the biographical data given on each lawyer to see if the lawyer's education or other data gives you any clues into personality or intellectual ability. You may, for example, favor a graduate of an Ivy League law school, or an attorney who has gone to your alma mater. This type of information is available in the *Martindale-Hubble Law Directory*.

9

LAWYERS WHO ADVERTISE

Prior to 1977, lawyers were not allowed to advertise. In 1977, the U. S. Supreme Court reversed the situation, granting to lawyers the right to advertise certain information in the media.

Why Advertising Is Good

We think that lawyer advertising, within the permitted guidelines, can be helpful to you if approached with care. It is another way to find a lawyer. It gives you a good idea of fees charged for specific, basic matters, and lets you compare fees for similar services. Be aware that advertisements usually only cover fees for uncomplicated matters, such as an uncontested divorce, a name change, or a simple will. If you have that type of problem, advertising will give you an idea of what is probably the lowest price for the service. If your problem is more complicated, advertising will give you a baseline figure from which fee negotiations can begin.

An Advertisement Is not a Guarantee

You should understand that an advertisement is meant to attract you and rarely tells you the full story. Always ask what is and is not included for the quoted price. Ask about extra charges—for photocopying, filing fees, paralegal time, and possibly many other items. If you don't ask, you may be in for a surprise when the bill arrives and the "extras" appear.

Ask for References

Finding a lawyer through an advertisement is obviously far less safe and dependable than finding one through personal references. But there are steps you can take to improve your odds.

Always ask an advertising lawyer for references and about his/her experience. Never hire a lawyer based on an advertisement without doing your best to check out the claims made.

When you interview the lawyer, take the advertisement with you. Ask in detail about the advertised service you require. How the lawyer responds to specific questions regarding the advertisement and his/her experience will, hopefully, give you some insight into the lawyer's personality and integrity.

10

CAN I DO IT MYSELF?

There are circumstances when you may think that you can conclude a legal matter yourself, especially in an area where you have acquired some experience. We agree, but we caution that it may be wise to have even a simple matter looked over by an experienced attorney as extra insurance.

For example, if you are about to sign a new employment contract, we strongly suggest that you discuss the details of the agreement with an attorney before you conclude negotiations for the deal. Similarly, if you are buying or selling a house, consult a real estate lawyer to make sure that your rights are protected in case of default by the other party or other problems. Using a lawyer for a brief consultation before problems arise often can save you time, heartache, and money later.

What about following the instructions on a pre-printed form or those in a do-it-yourself book? While people have certainly used these successfully in specific situations, they can be a dangerous substitute for the education and experience of a practicing attorney who is on your side. A lawyer can give you advice based on many years of specialized education and experience, and tailored to your own specific case. When you do it yourself, you do not have the advantage of expert guidance and you may become a victim of the old saying, "Anyone who represents him/herself has a fool for a client."

Small Claims Court

There are, however, certain circumstances where the law encourages you to act without an attorney. The first of these is the small claims court, where the legal system gives you the opportunity to settle minor, non-criminal problems without an attorney.

Small claims courts (which in some areas may be called municipal court, magistrate's court, or justice of the peace) are courts of law empowered to award monetary damages as compensation for wrongdoing. They have jurisdictional restrictions on the amount and type of claim that they handle. If your claim is over the dollar limit (which varies, according to locale, from $500 to $5,000), or if your claim is based on a problem which is outside the court's jurisdiction, then you will not be eligible for small claims court.

Small claims courts are usually excellent for resolving minor matters involving improper repairs, failure of a landlord to provide required services or refund a security deposit, breach of warranty, or other similar cases. You can check both the dollar limit and the jurisdiction (the types of cases handled by the small claims courts in your state) by telephoning the clerk of the court. The court's address can be found in the telephone book under the city or county listings, or you can call the local bar association for information.

The cost of filing in small claims court is usually small, and the amount of time you have to wait before your case is heard is usually brief. Some states allow you to be represented by an attorney, while others forbid professional representation.

Again, we stress that small claims courts are usually limited as to the amount of monetary damages that can be awarded. Also, if money won't solve your problem, then small claims is not for you. For example, if your neighbor's child keeps running his tricycle through your prize rose garden, the small claims court can order your neighbor to pay for the destroyed rose bushes. In most states, however, the court cannot order the neighbor to keep the child off your property.

Preparing Your Case

Before you go to small claims court, we strongly suggest that you try to resolve your dispute by writing letters to your opponent, detailing the problem and suggesting a reasonable solution, and, if it is appropriate, filing complaints with local agencies like the Better Business Bureau, Office of Consumer Protection, or Consumer Action Agency.

Make sure that you keep copies of your letters for your files. These will be most helpful when you present your case in court. In order to recover, you will have to show actual monetary loss detailed in some solid, documented way. For example, if your rose bushes have been destroyed, you will have to present sales receipts showing how much the rose bushes originally cost you or how much it will cost to replace them.

You will also have to prove that the other person was legally responsible for your loss and that you have tried to prevent additional damage to your property.

The small claims court will not expect you to know all that an attorney knows. However, in order for you to recover, you will have to prove to the judge (or, in some states, the jury) that you were injured by the defendant and that the defendant was legally responsible for the injury, and you will have to give evidence of the precise amount of your loss.

Appeal

Most, but not all, states allow the decisions of the small claims court to be appealed to a higher court. The appealability of a decision is up to the state, or possibly your opponent, and you should check with the court before filing your case regarding your rights of appeal.

Fill in the Blanks

Earlier in this chapter we referred briefly to another popular form of do-it-yourself law, the blank forms that you can fill in yourself. These forms are popularly available for many legal matters from a will or trust to a bankruptcy, incorporation, or divorce.

We strongly advise you to avoid blank forms because they simply can't address all individual issues. Moreover, they may ignore various contingencies of local ordinance and state law. True, the forms may adequately fit certain standard cases. But unless you consult with a lawyer, you may judge badly as to whether your own situation fits the standard mold or not.

For example, let's say that you are married and have no children. You might very well be suited for a simple form will leaving your entire estate to your spouse. But now let's say that you and your spouse were to die together in an automobile accident. What would happen to your estate? Unless the form you selected provided for (and you filled in) the name of an alternate beneficiary or beneficiaries, your estate would be disposed of according to the rules of your state, possibly going to relatives whom you would not have chosen if you had considered the matter.

Yes, the forms may work satisfactorily in some cases. But they can only handle the broadest categories and can't make allowances for individual circumstances and desires. You use them at your own risk.

Arbitration and Mediation

Arbitration and mediation are less costly and usually less time-consuming alternatives to going to court. Arbitration is usually by prior agreement; that is, it is written into many contracts, and is often used to settle commercial disputes. Arbitration may be binding or not, depending on the agreement of the parties

Arbitration, like small claims court, offers a simple and expeditious way of handling many problems. But arbitration offers much more flexibility than small claims court, and awards other than money can be made. In addition, most arbitration procedures do not have an upper monetary recovery limit.

Lawyers are often used in arbitrations, although

they aren't required. If your opponent has a lawyer, it is probably best for you to have one, too.

The most famous arbitration organization is the American Arbitration Association. Many states have court-sponsored arbitration programs as alternatives to small claims courts. Most arbitration programs have guidelines regarding the types of cases they handle.

Mediation is similar to arbitration, as both are noncourtroom methods of settling problems. However, mediation is not usually by prior agreement, but the result of both parties wanting to resolve their differences in an atmosphere that is fast and informal. Whether or not the results of mediation are appealable is determined before the procedure begins. Mediation is often used to resolve family matters, such as divorce settlements, although the service is used for other types of disputes as well. The mediator is similar to a referee. Unlike an arbitrator, who actually makes a decision, a mediator does not decide the case. Rather, he/she suggests ways for satisfactory resolution and helps the parties reach agreement.

Lawyers are sometimes used in mediation. As in arbitrations, if your opponent has a lawyer, it is probably best for you to have one, too.

Judicate, Inc.

Judicate, Inc. is a full-service private company offering a full range of judicial services in 38 states. Judicate is expanding rapidly and now employs almost 200 former state and federal judges to provide quick resolution of disputes through mediation, arbitration or trial. Speed of resolution and a reasonable fee for services are among its advantages. People who want fast and efficient service without the long delays that occur in most courts may decide to let Judicate handle their case.

The parties have the choice, depending on the type of case and the forum selected (trial, mediation, or arbitration), to have Judicate's decision binding or appealable. They also can choose whether or not to use lawyers to handle the case.

Judicate can be contacted by calling, toll-free, 1-800-631-9900. Another smaller, more limited service is offered by Dispute Resolution, Inc., in Hartford, Connecticut.

PART III—WHICH LAWYER TO CHOOSE

11

THE LAWYER'S QUALIFICATIONS

You may or may not be judged by the company you keep, but you will always be judged by the lawyer you hire. As a result, you must choose carefully and hire an attorney who conveys the image, attitude, and style you want to present to the world.

Before we discuss in detail which lawyer will be best for you, let us briefly describe a lawyer's training and background.

Education

In most states, before a person is allowed to take the bar examination, he/she must be a graduate of accredited undergraduate and law schools. Years ago, the schooling requirement varied greatly among the states, some not requiring an undergraduate degree but only several years of legal apprenticeship known as a clerkship or preceptorship. Now, the need to attend undergraduate and law schools is mandatory and the bar exam, once the bastion of each state, has taken on a national character as well.

However, unlike medicine, where the national exam means that a doctor can practice in any state desired, the national ("Multistate") bar exam does not automatically admit a lawyer to practice anywhere. Rather each state may also have an examination and/ or practical requirements which must be met.

Clerkships

Some graduating law students decide to postpone practicing law for between one and three years to clerk for a judge. A clerkship with a judge can be a valuable experience, giving the lawyer insight into the workings of the legal system and a feeling for courtroom technique that will benefit future clients.

Lawyer, Attorney, Counsellor, Solicitor

A lawyer is the general term used to signify someone learned in the law. Attorney, attorney at law, counsellor, counsellor at law, counsel, and solicitor are alternative names for the same profession.

In England, there is a difference between a barrister and solicitor: the barrister argues cases in courts, while the solicitor takes care of other legal matters. This distinction does not exist in the United States.

Diplomas, Diplomas Everywhere

When you enter a lawyer's office, you may be impressed by the number of diplomas and certificates displayed. A certificate showing admission to the bar of a state or federal court tells you nothing except that the lawyer has been admitted to practice in that court.

Diplomas that are more impressive include those recognizing graduation from a prestigious undergraduate or law school, membership on a law review (the school publication run by the outstanding students in each class), or awards based on merit or service.

Specialization

Many lawyers indicate that they specialize in a given area and may, in fact, limit their law practice to one defined field such as domestic relations, taxation, bankruptcy, etc. Until quite recently, patent law was the only legal specialization which had strict requirements before an attorney could hold him/herself out as a specialist. However, that is changing, and may states, including Texas, Florida, New Mexico, South Carolina, California, and Arizona, to name a few of the continually growing number, now have procedures for specialization certification.

The areas of specialization vary according to the state, with the following among the more common certifications: civil trial law, criminal law, estate planning and probate law, labor law, marital and family law (also known as domestic relations), personal injury trial law, real estate law, tax law, and workmen's compensation law. Your local bar association will tell you if attorneys in your area can be certified as specialists.

Patent Law

The one area in which lawyers traditionally have been certified as specialists is patent law. To practice before the U.S. Patent Office, a lawyer must fulfill two requirements. First, he/she must display adequate legal, scientific, and technical ability. This usually means a technical undergraduate degree (in engineering or physics, for example), or sufficient courses or practical experience to prove the lawyer able to render technical assistance to a patent applicant. Second, an examination must be passed focusing on the rules of patent application, prosecution, and appeal.

Officer of the Court

An attorney is an officer of the court, sworn to uphold the Constitution and the laws to protect the rights of his/her client. Note that this means that the lawyer has certain obligations to the court and the law, and not only to the client.

Confidentiality

However, the law recognizes the special importance of the lawyer-client relationship. In general, whatever is said between a lawyer and his/her client is totally confidential. The exceptions to this rule of confidentiality are few. For example, you may freely tell your attorney of a crime you may have committed in the past. In fact, revealing such information may be absolutely necessary in preparing your defense. But, if you tell your lawyer that you are going to commit a crime in the future, the lawyer may have to inform the authorities, as information regarding plans for the future commission of a crime has been held not to be confidential. In addition, Pennsylvania courts have recently held that an attorney may have to reveal the location of an absent defendant if the client's absence interferes with the administration of justice.

Paralegal

A paralegal is a trained legal assistant who earns less than a lawyer and whose services are billed to clients at lower rates, saving time for the lawyer and saving money for the client. A paralegal doesn't appear in court and is not qualified to give legal advice, but assists a lawyer by filling out and filing necessary documents and papers and organizing case files and other information for the lawyer. In general, the efficient use of paralegals is an indication of a well-run law firm.

Paralegals in large cities often have some specialized legal education. In many areas, however, paralegals learn by experience, working under the supervision of an attorney until they are qualified to handle certain matters on their own.

12

BIG FIRM, SMALL FIRM, OR SOLE PRACTITIONER?

Some lawyers practice alone, others in small groups, still others as part of a large firm. In this chapter we will discuss some of the advantages and disadvantages of each type of practice from the standpoint of you, the client.

How Big Is Big?

First, let us point out that size is relative. A sole practitioner is a sole practitioner wherevcr he/she practices. But what is considered a small or a large firm may vary according to the location. In Bangor, Maine, for example, the largest firm has 26 lawyers, while in Philadelphia, Pennsylvania, the largest firm has over 350 lawyers. A New York law firm can have over 100 attorneys and be considered of medium size. There's no absolute standard.

Partner or Associate

Before we discuss the advantages and disadvantages of large and small firms, a word on law firm nomenclature.

When a young lawyer joins a firm, he/she becomes an "associate," that is, someone associated with, but not yet part of, the firm. After many years of hard work, the associate may be asked to become a "partner" in the firm.

A partner is a full member of the firm, sharing responsibility for the firm's actions and sharing in the partnership earnings. If the law firm is a corporation, rather than a partnership, the associate becomes a shareholder rather than a partner; the terminology is different, but the result is the same.

Of Counsel

Many firms use the term "Of Counsel" to indicate an attorney affiliated with the firm but not actually a member of it. This term is often used to honor a distinguished civil servant who has returned to practice law after a career as, for example, a public prosecutor or judge. It may also be applied to an older partner who has withdrawn from full participation in the firm.

Advantages of a Big Firm

Big firms are excellent for big clients or big problems. If your problem crosses many different areas of the law, a large firm will give you the diversity of specialization and variety of lawyers and experience to match the complexity of your case, whatever it may be.

Big firms are often especially good for business clients. If you own a business, a large firm can easily handle your tax problems, securities registration, labor negotiations, and real estate acquisitions without the need to go to specialized firms in each area.

An individual may also choose a big firm, for several possible reasons. First, big firms carry prestige. If you want status, and are willing to pay the price, a big firm is for you.

Second, if your problem is complex, such as handling an inheritance which includes cash, jewelry, and real estate, the diverse resources of a large firm will be very helpful.

Finally, if the recommendations of lawyers you have gotten from friends, etc., prove not to your liking, you may want to go to a big firm where you can be reasonably assured of good quality work and the maintenance of relatively high standards.

Is Bigger Better?

As noted above, there are two main advantages to a large firm. The first is the quality of law practiced and the second is the diversity of specializations.

Traditionally, large law firms have been able to attract the best and the brightest graduating legal talent because of their reputations and prestige, because they pay starting attorneys more money, and because they hold out the hope of eventual very high income and high prestige at the partnership level. For example, the large New York law firms are paying top law graduates starting salaries of $65,000 or more per year. These salaries are made possible by the high fees paid by clients of the large firms. Smaller firms generally can't meet this competition for the top graduates.

Does this mean that the best lawyers can only be found in the biggest firms? Absolutely not; experience is an important factor in judging an attorney's ability, and there is more to a good lawyer than good grades in law school. But one thing is clear—on the whole, the law graduates with the best grades are most likely to be found in the larger firms.

Because of their organization, continuity, and access to top talent, the quality of the law practiced in the larger firms tends to be high. You may receive equally fine service from a small firm or sole practitioner, but if you don't have a dependable recommendation and can't afford to experiment, you can be more assured of quality work at a large firm.

Large firms are also better able to handle complicated problems because of the many different areas of specialization within the firm. The largest firms generally have separate sections specializing in litigation, tax, estates, corporate work, and real estate, as well as other possible specialties.

Disadvantages of Big Firms

The main disadvantage of a big firm is the cost. Big firms charge more in general than small firms or sole practitioners (excepting some highly paid sole specialists). A large firm has high overhead costs including paralegals, secretaries, messengers, rent, word processing equipment, a research library, and a host of other costs. You are often paying for review of the work at two or more levels. And the fees are calculated to include high salaries for both partners and associates.

The second disadvantage of a big firm is the tendency of smaller clients either to get lost in the shuffle or to be relegated to the newest associate. If your case will not generate big fees, chances of your getting the services of one of the senior partners are low. You are then faced with the dilemma of deciding whether to use a junior partner or associate in a large firm, or a more experienced attorney at a smaller firm.

Advantages of a Small Firm

A good small firm with an excellent reputation can often give you fine service and cost you less money than a large firm. Small firms are more personalized. If your problems are not particularly complex and do not require many different types of legal specialists, a high quality small firm may give you extra attention and permit you to develop a more personal rapport with your attorney. And some smaller firms do include lawyers with various specialties, though the range of experience can hardly match that at the larger firms.

Disadvantages of a Small Firm

Whether the lesser depth and diversification at a small firm matters to you will depend in part on the nature of your legal problems. Obviously, it is unlikely that five or ten attorneys will know as much as 50, 100, or 200. It is less certain in a smaller firm that someone will have handled a case similar to yours during their careers. And if one attorney is unavailable for any reason, it is less certain that another attorney with similar experience will be available to step in and fill the gap.

If you are choosing a smaller firm, think twice before basing your judgment on which firm charges the lowest fees. A small firm with a low fee schedule may be under pressure to represent many small clients in order to make ends meet. In such a case, while the largest clients usually continue to get good service, the smaller clients may run the risk of getting lost in the crowd.

Advantages of a Sole General Practitioner

A sole general practitioner is the family doctor of the legal profession. This type of attorney usually practices by him/herself or sometimes in a group of nonaffiliated lawyers sharing office space. Most sole general practitioners tend to concentrate on serving individuals or small businesses. If personal rapport is important to you and if you do not think that you need a specialist to handle your problems, then finding a compatible sole general practitioner may be like discovering a new and trusted friend.

The sole general practitioner is excellent for people who don't have complex legal problems, but who need a lawyer occasionally for routine legal matters such as writing a basic will or buying or selling a home. In these personal matters a capable, experienced sole generalist may be exactly the right choice.

Personal attention and a personalized relationship are the greatest advantages of having a sole general practitioner on your side. A sole practitioner who becomes your "family lawyer" and learns about your personal situations over the years may become a valued advisor on more than strictly legal matters.

Two words of warning: first, as we said in regard to the smaller firms, be wary of a sole practitioner who charges very low fees and then takes on too many clients in order to compensate. In this case, you won't get the good personal service you're looking for.

Second, make sure that your sole practitioner is willing to refer you to a specialist when such expertise is needed. A sole practitioner who resists this type of decision can't be relied on. No lawyer can be expert on everything, and a good lawyer will be frank about his/her limitations.

Disadvantages of a Sole General Practitioner

We have already touched on some of the disadvantages associated with using a sole general practitioner. Obviously, a sole practitioner who has a general practice of law cannot possibly be as expert or as current on various areas of the law as can someone who specializes.

A sole generalist probably will not have the paralegal, research, and technical backup that a larger group enjoys.

A sole generalist in need of fees may take on so many cases that giving adequate attention promptly to each case becomes impossible.

A sole generalist may charge you a lower rate per hour and yet not save you money, since the lawyer's lack of specialized knowledge may necessitate more time-consuming research.

When to Use a Sole Specialist

A sole specialist is an attorney who limits his/her practice to one area of the law. Specialists exist in many areas including criminal, plaintiff's injury, entertainment, patent, divorce, and labor law.

If your problem is complex but falls within one discrete area of the law, a high quality sole specialist may be your answer. For example, if you want to obtain a divorce, the divorce settlement might be complex and might cover such varied legal areas as taxes, trusts, real estate and insurance. It might seem at first blush that you would need the services of many different lawyers to handle all the areas involved. A good divorce specialist, however, would be expert on many of these areas as they relate to the problems of divorce.

Another example is entertainment law. Someone in the arts may have questions regarding copyright, trademark, contract, tax, insurance, and other legal areas. Rather than hiring an expert in each field, an artist will hire an entertainment lawyer whose expertise includes the application of these disciplines to the problems of the arts and entertainment industries.

Advantages of a Sole Specialist

The sole specialist is a team of lawyers in one convenient package.

The advantage of a sole specialist, very simply, is that an attorney who practices only one type of law will ordinarily be more expert in that particular type of practice, and more knowledgeable about any changes in the law that might affect your situation.

Disadvantages of a Sole Specialist

The first disadvantage of a sole specialist is that you may need another attorney to handle any problems you have that don't fall within the specialty area.

The second disadvantage is that a sole specialist will usually charge more per hour, or, if a contingency fee is involved, may demand a higher percentage fee (see Chapter 17). Remember, however, that while a sole specialist may charge more hourly, the fact that he/she is expert in the area will mean that he/she can accomplish more in less time, and with less new research. So, while your hourly fee may be higher than with a sole generalist or with the average small firm, your total bill may not be higher.

13

"STOREFRONT" LAW FIRMS

Storefront law firms are the modern country lawyers. Many urban and suburban areas have storefront law firms, also known as neighborhood law offices or legal clinics. They should not, however, be confused with legal aid or federally subsidized legal clinics. The storefront firms deliver legal services for a full, if less costly, fee.

In general, you should treat storefront lawyers like any other lawyers, giving credit for convenience and being careful to judge each lawyer on his/her merits, experience, and suitability to your particular needs.

Storefront National Law Firms

There is one new variety of storefront law firm that needs separate discussion, and that is the new "storefront national" law firms that are spreading across the country. The largest of these is Hyatt Legal Services.

Several firms of this type have been expanding rapidly, either by taking over similarly situated law practices or by opening new offices on their own, and can be found in most major cities. Most of their clients come through television, radio, and newspaper advertisements.

These firms should not be confused with the more traditional national law firms which have offices in several cities and/or states. All offices of a traditional firm are strongly interconnected, sharing clients and billings as part of their structure. While the storefront national law firm is centrally administered, the use of an attorney in one of their offices gives only slightly

50

greater access to another office in another city or state. Clients are not shared, and the offices in many respects operate autonomously.

What Is Offered?

Storefront national firms offer complete law firm services at local, easily accessible offices by staff attorneys. A full range of services is offered, ranging from wills to criminal defense.

Who Are the Attorneys?

Frequently, young attorneys with little experience work at storefront national firms as a first job or to gain experience. As the salaries cannot compete with those offered by traditional law firms, the more successful law students do not tend to practice with these firms. However, the firms do have experienced supervisory attorneys with specialized knowledge of the firm's most frequently provided services.

Turnover

There is a marked turnover of lawyers at these firms, with the average stay substantially less than one year. The turnover stems from a variety of reasons, including monthly earning goals and high caseloads. An attorney may be asked to leave if his/her monthly earning goals are not met.

This turnover can create problems for a client whose case lasts more than a few months, because the attorney originally hired may not be there when the case is finally concluded.

A related problem is that when you pay your initial fee, the attorney whom you meet when you hire the firm is credited with the revenue. When that attorney leaves, another attorney will be assigned to your case. However, the new lawyer will not be credited with previously paid sums, so the incentive for the second attorney is missing, as he/she still has monthly revenue goals to consider.

51

What Is the Fee?

Storefront nationals pride themselves on being able to offer legal services at reduced rates. They accomplish this by using paralegals to process routine paperwork and by working in volume. They frequently charge a flat fee for services; however, additionally required services may raise the cost substantially.

A detailed contract regarding fees will be signed by you and by the staff attorney before any work is begun. The contract will also detail the hourly rate to be charged for services not included in the flat fee. As of the writing of this book, the hourly fee charged by these firms averaged about $100.

Certain services—like the writing of a basic will, a personal bankruptcy, a child custody hearing, or a basic incorporation—carry fees that are significantly lower than those which would be charged by most other lawyers. These firms make their money on volume, and so can afford to charge less per routine item. However, when complications arise, the final bill can be high, because additional attorney time required for a complex matter will be billed at the hourly rate.

These firms also work on a contingency fee arrangement for cases such as personal injury or workmen's compensation. The fee for personal injury matters averages approximately 40% of the recovery. However, unlike most private attorneys who will either advance or absorb the cost of expert witnesses and other expenses in a contingency situation, some storefront nationals require you to pay for them up front. (See Chapter 17.)

A minimum amount, usually $250 or so, must be paid after you sign the fee agreement in order to open your file. The balance of the contracted amount, including any overages and fees for expenses, must be paid before the firm will conclude your case by filing the final papers. Money for additional services must be paid before those services are begun.

Are Fees Negotiable?

Technically, the answer is no, but in reality, there is some room for negotiation, depending on the individual attorney. The amount of the flat fee and the hourly fee are not negotiable. However, the payment terms are usually left up to the individual attorney. How many services you get for your flat fee is also partly negotiable, and if you are lucky, a particularly accommodating lawyer might give you two support hearings for the price of one.

When to Use Them

Following is a list of areas in which we find the storefront nationals proficient: name change; standard will with limited estate planning; uncontested/no-fault divorce with limited property division; child custody or support problems; basic incorporation (without subchapter S or other election); fictitious name filing; or basic personal bankruptcy.

The storefront nationals are acceptable choices for these and some other basic legal matters. We do not recommend them generally for complicated problems because the turnover in legal staff limits continuity of supervision, and the volume of cases handled by each attorney may restrict high level individual attention and service.

The Pitch

You will find that, when you go to one of these firms, you will receive "the pitch," somewhat like the pitch you would receive if you were to buy a used car or sign up for dancing lessons. The pitch is fast-paced and encouraging. Think carefully before you sign on the dotted line.

Is the Lower Price Worth It?

The answer depends on your problem and your desires. If you want to establish a continuing relationship with an attorney who will be there to help you in the future, the answer is no. These attorneys do not usually remain at the firm for a long time. If you have a problem that basically involves filing legal documents, then the answer might very well be yes, because you can get the same legal services for less money.

National Attention

As we said earlier, each office or region of a storefront national firm is largely autonomous. Aside from a telephone call to another office, they are not structured to work together in a traditional sense, nor do they share clients. If you need a referral to a lawyer in another state, you might do better by calling the local bar association's lawyer reference service. (See Chapter 8.)

14

THE "REASONABLE" LAWYER

The Reasonable Lawyer is a *No-Nonsense* concept we use to describe an attorney who is capable, experienced, intelligent, considerate, and involved. No, we are not describing a Boy Scout or Girl Scout. The reasonable lawyer is a real attorney whom you can find if you look seriously and intelligently.

The word "reasonable" has special meaning in certain areas of the law. We won't get into legal theory, except to note that the law assumes that most people have a common understanding of what "reasonable" means.* We agree with that, and think that "reasonable" is a useful word to apply to the choice of a lawyer. Following are some characteristics of the reasonable lawyer.

The Reasonable Lawyer Speaks English

Don't be intimidated by Latin. "Legalese" comes in large part from Latin—a "dead" language which, in our opinion, is best left dead and not spoken. Granted, many Latin terms are used in court pleadings, briefs, and other documents, but if you find an attorney who only speaks in *res ipse loquiturs*, *ipso factos*, and *corpus*

---

* The word "reasonable" holds high significance in the law. The standard for guilt in the criminal law, as readers may know from the Perry Mason series and other courtroom fiction, is guilt "beyond a reasonable doubt"—not beyond *all* doubt, but only beyond a *reasonable* doubt. Similarly, the standard for determining tort liability in civil cases is whether a "reasonable person" in similar circumstances would have acted as the defendant acted; if the answer is yes, there is no liability.

juris secundums—you have not found the reasonable lawyer.

On the other hand, if you find an attorney who does speak in legalese but explains the meaning of each term so that you understand it, you are doing well in your reasonable lawyer search.

The Reasonable Lawyer Listens to You

> The Law is the true embodiment
> Of everything that's excellent
> It has no kind of fault or flaw,
> And I, my Lords, embody the Law.

Sir W. S. Gilbert, Iolanthe

In a lawyer, the ability to listen is as essential as the ability to communicate clearly. The reasonable lawyer isn't pompous. A lawyer who wants to hear him/herself talk, on your time and at your expense, is one to avoid. Of course, once you have explained your problem, you expect a lawyer to take some time to explain possible solutions, problems, and courses of action; that's entirely different from being bombastic on your dollar. But you want a lawyer who will talk *with* you and not *at* you. A lawyer who doesn't respond clearly to your questions or comments should be avoided.

The Reasonable Lawyer May not Have All the Answers Immediately

Don't be put off if a lawyer tells you that he/she doesn't know the answer to your particular problem immediately. This might conceivably be a way of increasing your fee by forcing another visit, but it may be legitimate. Complex or novel problems often can't be answered without a certain amount of research. If a lawyer is satisfactory in other respects, the fact that he/she doesn't have all the answers on the tip of the tongue may be a sign of honesty that is to be respected.

The Reasonable Lawyer Returns Phone Calls Promptly

No lawyer is acceptable if he/she doesn't return your phone calls within 24 hours (provided, of course, that you haven't become a pest by phoning too frequently). There is one exception to this rule, and that is when an attorney is busy in court. If the receptionist or secretary indicates that your attorney is in court and will not be able to return your call for a day or two—accept that as long as the call is actually returned when promised. When a trial is actually in progress, a good attorney will often devote every available minute to it—as you would want your attorney to do if it were your case that was on trial.

Where Reputation Counts

Respect of one's peers is the highest compliment, and lawyers are generally shrewd judges of other lawyers. The reasonable lawyer will have an excellent reputation with other members of the bar.

Knowing One's Limitations

A good lawyer is wise enough not to try to be expert at everything. Knowing your own limitations and when to obtain the assistance of a specialist is a mark of the reasonable lawyer.

Objectivity

Sometimes a client is so emotionally entangled in a problem that acting logically becomes impossible. The reasonable lawyer is an objective observer who will help you see your problem more clearly and accurately.

This means that if you have illusions, your lawyer should not cater to them. It is essential for you to know the real merits of your case and what your attorney views as your chances of success. Remember that any evaluation your attorney gives you does not mean that he/she will not act as a devoted advocate in your behalf. But a reasonable lawyer will always try to show you the weaknesses in your case and the strengths in your opponent's case so that you are not faced with sudden disappointment later on. If a lawyer lays out a "worst case scenario" and then tells you that, in spite of it, he/she thinks you have a pretty good chance of prevailing—you may have found a reasonable lawyer.

If a lawyer promises you the world or says that your opponent doesn't have a chance—be wary. If, however, several lawyers agree, you have reason to be optimistic.

Remember that objectivity involves what we often refer to simply as good common sense. If a lawyer does not have this quality, all the legal brilliance in the world may prove useless.

The Reasonable Lawyer Is not Litigation Happy

The only certainty where litigation is concerned is that the lawyers involved will earn large fees. The results of litigation are always uncertain, and the toll of time, emotional strain, and money can be very difficult.

The reasonable lawyer will look for opportunities for a negotiated settlement before filing a lawsuit and, even after a suit has been filed, will continue to look for opportunities for a fair settlement before the case actually goes to trial.

Sometimes, of course, a trial can't be avoided. But beware of the lawyer who doesn't seek diligently to avoid it.

The Reasonable Lawyer Is Trustworthy

Your secrets are just that—yours. The reasonable lawyer will live up to his/her professional responsibilities by protecting your privacy and acting as a trustworthy guardian of your confidences.

15

THE INTERVIEW

Once you have compiled a list of several possible lawyers to use, try to take the time to interview each of them. It is always best to speak to several attorneys before making your selection, especially if the problems you expect to deal with are serious or complex. Remember that the choice of a lawyer is a very personal matter and too important to leave to the opinion of someone else.

What to Look For

The two most important words to remember are *rapport* and *confidence*. You must feel that you can talk with your lawyer comfortably and that he/she understands your problems and feelings. You must also have confidence in the lawyer—confidence in his/her experience, judgment, and understanding of your problem, and also in the lawyer's ability to represent you before the world.

Setting Up the Interview

Telephone each lawyer on your list and ask to make an appointment for a consultation regarding possible representation. Always ask whether there will be a charge for this initial visit. Many lawyers will meet with you for a half hour or an hour to discuss representation without charging a fee for the initial interview. Some charge a small fee.

You Are the Boss

This is the time for you to interview the attorney. Don't be intimidated by fancy offices, legal mumbo-jumbo, or pomposity. Remember the characteristics of the reasonable lawyer (Chapter 14). Your job is to determine if the person you are interviewing fits those standards and meets your personal needs.

You should not be seeking legal advice during this interview (although you will probably get some for free). The interview is the time to tell the attorney about your case, to discuss the attorney's ability to represent you, and to explore your possible courses of action.

Write a Chronology

Before the interview, if you are seeking advice and representation for a specific case, write a chronology of the events relevant to the case. Otherwise, simply write down the reasons why you are seeking legal advice. During the interview, you can either read this list to the lawyer or give it to him/her to read. This will save time and get you more quickly into the real substance of the interview.

Be Honest

You must be frank, open, and honest during this initial interview. The lawyer can understand your position only if he/she knows the relevant facts. Don't withhold significant information because you are embarrassed. The lawyer can't assess the merits of your case if some of the facts are missing. Relax and forget your embarrassment; lawyers are trained not to be moralists, but to analyze the facts of a case objectively and without assessing fault.

Ten *No-Nonsense* Questions To Ask At The Interview

There is no one right way to conduct the interview. You should try to let the conversation flow in directions that tell you as much as possible about the lawyer. Here are specific questions to ask which will help you get the information you want:

1. What is your educational background?
2. What is your main area of expertise?
3. How many cases like mine have you handled? How recently? What were the results?
4. Will you personally handle my case, or will someone else in the firm?
5. How do you estimate my chances of success?
6. How long do you think it will take to conclude this matter?
7. What is your normal procedure when dealing with clients? Will I get copies of all paperwork? When can I telephone you? Do you have evening or weekend hours? How long will I have to wait to get another appointment?
8. Do you employ paralegals? Will they work on my case, and will their use reduce the amount of my bill?
9. How much and on what basis do you charge? What do you estimate my final bill will be? Can I have an estimate of additional costs and a sample of what your bill will look like?
10. Why should I choose you over the other lawyers that have been recommended to me?

Prior Experience

Ask the attorney about prior experience in the area of the law where you are seeking assistance. Note carefully questions 2 and 3 above. Don't be afraid to ask those questions, simply and directly. Remember that a reasonable lawyer will not push to handle a case in an area where he/she cannot function at a high level of competence.

Asking for References

If you have obtained the attorney's name from a lawyers' reference service or through some other impersonal recommendation, and not from the personal experience of someone you know and trust, ask if you can speak to a client. Obviously, the lawyer will only give you the name of a satisfied client who is expected to speak well of the lawyer, but even such a conversation should give you some insight into the lawyer's character and way of working.

Keep in mind that many attorneys are reluctant to disclose the names of any clients. You probably should not hold this guarding of confidentiality against the lawyer, especially if you are comfortable with him/her in other areas.

Fees

We will discuss fee arrangements fully in Part IV. Here, we want only to point out that fees must be fully discussed in the interview.

Ask about the attorney's hourly rate, the terms of a contingency fee, and the possibility of a flat fee. Ask which services and expenses are included in the fee and which are not. Ask how expenses are assigned to you. Some firms add a flat fee for expenses to all bills, while others charge you on the basis of work performed. Which one is best for you depends on the nature of your case.

Ask also how the services of others in the firm, such as junior lawyers and/or paralegals, will be billed and at what rate.

Ask About Procedure

During the initial interview, the attorney should give you some general suggestions about how to proceed with your case. Don't expect detailed recommendations; not all the facts have been presented, and there has been no time for the lawyer to think, research, or consider. However, an experienced attorney should be able to tell you something immediately about the potential problems and possible solutions, especially if he/she is expert in the area.

You should also ask the lawyer specifically to describe his/her procedure regarding settling claims. It is important for the lawyer to understand that you are the one to make the final decision regarding any settlement. You should not give an attorney broad discretion to settle a claim until you know and trust the attorney and are sure that his/her judgment is sound and in tune with yours.

Who Will Handle Your Case?

Ask the attorney who will effectively be in charge of your case—the lawyer him/herself, a junior partner, or an associate. Ask to what extent the work will actually be done by each of these and to what extent by paralegals. Ask how billings are apportioned among the legal staff who work on your problem. Make sure that you will not be billed at a senior partner's hourly rate for work that was actually accomplished by a junior partner or associate.

Conflicts of Interest

A "conflict of interest" situation exists when a lawyer either represents parties with opposing interests, or has knowledge of facts that the rule of confidentiality prevents disclosing to a client.

Some conflicts are obvious. For example, an attorney cannot represent both parties in a bitterly contested divorce. The goals of the two spouses will be different and often opposite, making it impossible for one attorney to be an advocate for both sides.

On the other hand, suppose a husband and wife are getting a divorce they both want? There are no children, and all the property has been amicably divided. Can they both use the same lawyer to file the necessary paperwork?

The answer is not as simple as it may appear. The first answer is yes, they can both use the same lawyer. But should they? Probably not. Any competent lawyer they speak to will point out the potential conflicts between the parties and will probably not represent them both without making each sign an agreement waiving possible claims and agreeing to be represented by the same attorney.

Obviously, if your problem involves a potential lawsuit, any relationship between your lawyer and any *potentially* adversary party will be unacceptable.

When it comes to avoiding conflicts of interest, some lawyers take a stricter approach than others. What if you give a brief description of your problem, naming other parties who may be opposing you in a potential lawsuit, and the attorney says that there doesn't seem to be a conflict "at this time," or other similar words? Don't let the matter rest there. You certainly don't want to hire a lawyer and work with him/her, only to find later that the lawyer has to withdraw because of a conflict of interest. Ask for an explanation of the potential problems. If there is any possibility of conflict—look for another lawyer to help you with this problem.

16

THE BARRACUDA AND THE AMBULANCE CHASER

Lawyers come with reputations that can be described in numerous ways—brilliant, kind, considerate, tough, cunning, dirty, sleazy, shrewd, understanding, etc. There are, however, two types of lawyers we feel deserve special mention—the "barracuda" and the "ambulance chaser."

The Barracuda

A "barracuda" is an attorney with a reputation for overly aggressive ruthlessness—one who goes for the jugular in all cases, justifiably or not. A barracuda makes the opposition miserable. That's what he/she is paid to do. Barracudas are most prominent in areas of the law where emotions run high, such as divorce.

The Monetary Cost

This type of highly aggressive lawyer is usually very costly because his/her tactics tend to prolong problems rather than solve them amicably. In cases where barracuda tactics are justified, you will pay dearly for this particular type of expertise.

The Emotional Cost

Worse than the monetary cost is the emotional drain of hiring a barracuda. These lawyers play on the nerves and emotions of the opposition, and sometimes on those of the client as well. Only hire a barracuda if you have the stomach for it.

Does It Take a Barracuda to Fight a Barracuda?

If the opposition has hired a barracuda, you may feel obliged to hire one in self-defense. Sometimes this is a necessary tactic. But we caution you that it is often more effective to fight a barracuda with a reasonable lawyer as described in Chapter 14. The expertise and knowledge of a competent professional can often throw an overly aggressive lawyer off the track and bring matters to a quick resolution.

Making the Opposition Suffer

Many people hire barracudas when they want their opponent to suffer and don't care how much it costs or how agonizing the experience will be. As we said, this is often true in emotionally charged areas of the law, such as divorce.

Conclusion

In our opinion, it is usually better to hire a reasonable lawyer who might be able to work things out fairly than it is to prolong the problem by hiring a barracuda. However, if you are set on punishing your opponent, or if you feel that you are fighting a losing battle against a ruthless opposition, and if you can afford the monetary and emotional cost, then you may want a barracuda.

The Ambulance Chaser

The "ambulance chaser" is another type of lawyer we generally recommend avoiding. These attorneys get business by physically pursuing accident victims. The ambulance chaser tends to haunt emergency rooms, often getting referrals from police, hospital, or ambulance staff (who usually get a "present" from the attorney for the referral).

If you have been injured and a lawyer appears magically without being asked, or if you are handed a lawyer's card by someone who knows that you have been injured—be careful. You may interview the lawyer if you wish, but you should also interview other candidates. If the ambulance chaser were good enough to attract clients by referrals from satisfied clients or from other attorneys, he/she presumably would not need to chase accident victims.

PART IV—FEES

My learned profession I'll never disgrace
By taking a fee with a grin on my face,
When I haven't been there to attend to the case.

Sir W. S. Gilbert, Iolanthe

17

FLAT, HOURLY, OR CONTINGENCY FEE?

Lawyers cost money. And the amount a lawyer charges is based on many factors, including experience, reputation, specialization, and market conditions.

Types of Fees

There are three basic ways of paying an attorney—a flat fee for a particular procedure or problem, by the hour, or on contingency. The method of billing used usually depends on the type of case, although there is little consistency in this area. If one type of billing is preferable to you, you may wish to shop around until you find a lawyer who will handle your problem on that fee basis.

Hourly Rate

Lawyers most commonly bill according to the time a particular matter takes to complete. The basis for billing is the individual lawyer's hourly rate.

Hourly rates are a function of status, experience, age, expertise, and market conditions. The time of a senior partner in a large law firm will be billed at a higher hourly rate than the time of a junior partner or associate. Large firms generally charge higher hourly rates than most small firm lawyers or sole generalists. Billing rates vary greatly with geography and other factors, but can range from as low as $50 per hour for a young sole practitioner to over $300 per hour for a leading partner in a major firm.

With an hourly rate, the lawyer is paid for the actual time spent working on your case. Lawyers call the time spent "billable" time, that is hours which are billable to the client.

The Six-Minute Dilemma

The larger the firm, or the more computerized, the smaller the increments of billable time. For example, many sole practitioners bill in segments of one-quarter hour. That is, if the hourly fee is $125.00, 30 minutes of time will cost $62.50 and 15 minutes, $31.25. Others bill in smaller segments, sometimes every tenth of an hour (6 minutes). It may seem to you that billing small intervals will make the lawyer a timekeeper instead of an attorney. The problem is real, but consider that if the billable segments are narrow, your bills will be more accurate. It is certainly better not to be billed for 15 minutes of time when you have had a 6-minute phone call.

If your lawyer bills in 15-minute intervals and you speak with him/her on the telephone for 20 minutes, will your bill be for one-quarter of an hour or one-half? The answer depends on the practice of the individual attorney or firm, and this is a reasonable question to ask before you agree to hire a lawyer.

The Flat Fee

A flat fee is a precise charge for performing one defined legal job. If your problem is a simple one, such as writing a will, filing a document, or negotiating a simple contract, a lawyer may offer to charge you a flat fee for the service. Flat fees are common for uncontested divorces, name change petitions, basic incorporations, house purchase or sale, and other similar, matters.

In the case of a flat fee, you must understand specifically what is included in the service and what is not. We again emphasize the importance of understanding clearly, at the beginning, what work is going to be performed, in order to avoid trouble or misunderstanding later.

For example, if you have agreed to pay a flat fee for an uncontested divorce and suddenly problems arise with your soon-to-be ex-spouse, the flat fee arrangement may end, and the attorney may begin to bill you hourly, unless you have made some other arrangement. Or, before the case began, you might have foreseen this possibility and agreed that if a custody or support hearing was required, you would be billed an additional specific amount.

On simple matters, you can check the reasonableness of a flat fee to a certain extent by comparing it to the fees stated in advertisements. But remember that you may not be comparing like services, since different extras may be included or excluded. Don't be surprised or offended if a good lawyer quotes a fee higher than some of the advertised figures, which are often kept artificially low.

Percentage Fees

Another type of fee is the percentage fee. This arrangement is common in estate cases, but we find little to say in its favor. With a percentage fee, the lawyer is paid a specific percentage of the value of the items he/she is dealing with. For example, the lawyer for a $600,000 estate might charge 4% of the value, or $24,000. If the estate had been worth $300,000, the time spent might well have been the same, but the lawyer would have received $12,000 for the work. As we believe that lawyers should be compensated for work actually performed, we do not favor percentage fees.

Contingency Fees

A contingency fee may look at first like a percentage fee, but it is quite different. With a contingency fee, a lawyer is paid out of the recovery a client receives on a case—if there is a recovery. The maximum amount of the contingency fee, which may be 25%, 40%, 50%, or more, is often set by state law.

In a contingency arrangement, the lawyer only

gets paid a fee if you win your case. His/her fee is contingent on victory and on a monetary award.

In this situation, you will no doubt have to sign a contingency fee agreement. Make sure that you understand the agreement and that it clearly spells out who will pay court costs, expert witness costs, and other costs. These are negotiable items, sometimes paid by the lawyer, sometimes by the client. Be aware that while you will not have to pay the lawyer's fee if you lose your case, your other costs may still be substantial. Try to get an estimate of these costs.

Lawyers commonly work on a contingency basis in personal injury and workmen's compensation cases. In certain states, contingency percentages are set by law or court rule. In other states, lawyers' fees in general are regulated by statute, while in some states only fees for certain types of cases are so regulated. Your local bar association can tell you how fees are regulated in your area.

Are Fees Negotiable?

Many lawyers' fees are negotiable. However, the degree of negotiability depends on the attorney involved, the type of case, the potential recovery, and other factors.

You can't force a lawyer to reduce his/her fee. You can try to reason with the lawyer, pointing out mitigating factors such as your financial limitations or the fact that another attorney offered to take the case for a lower fee.

You should definitely be able to negotiate the payment schedule. When you pay and how much is due at each installment are matters on which most lawyers will show some flexibility.

And finally, if the lawyer requests a retainer, the amount of the retainer is almost always negotiable.

When Estimates Are Needed

While vagueness on the part of a lawyer as to costs and fees is generally not acceptable, some problems are so complicated and uncertain that an accurate estimate is impossible. In that case, ask the lawyer for a range rather than a simple figure, or ask for a set of estimates based on different contingencies. For example, if the lawyer thinks it possible to settle your case, he/she might give an estimate based on a certain number of hours of work in discussions with the opposing parties and in drafting settlement documents. Or, if the case doesn't settle, and litigation is necessary, the lawyer could indicate the cost of trial preparation and the additional cost if the trial actually takes place. (Most lawyers charge more money for court time than for office time.) The lawyer might even give you an estimate of the costs if the matter is taken on appeal to a higher court.

What Does the Fee Include?

Whether your fee is set on an hourly, flat, or contingency basis, remember that there are no set rules regarding what is included in the fee. You must determine whether photocopying, telephone expense, postage, filing fees, expert witnesses or advice, and any other work not specifically performed by the lawyer or someone in his/her office is covered by the stated fee, or whether you will be billed extra for these items.

Who Will Handle Your Case?

If you are paying a high hourly fee for a senior partner in a large firm, make sure that you get what you are paying for—and not the services of a young associate or paralegal at senior partner prices. You have the right to ask for and receive detailed billings indicating who has actually worked on your case.

What if you suspect, later on, that you are being handled by someone other than the person whose services you are being billed for? Be direct—go into your lawyer's office and ask specifically who performed certain tasks. This may not endear you to your attorney, but hopefully it will ensure fair billing in the future.

How Do I Pay?

The timing of payments may be critical to you, especially if the total bill is large. Make sure you understand at the beginning just when you will be expected to make payments.

The cleanest procedure for an ongoing matter, and one which will nip any misunderstanding in the bud, is to receive a fully itemized bill at least once a month. You should also request a receipt for each payment.

Some attorneys accept credit cards, some will take a check, while others will only accept a certified check, money order, or cash.

Retainers

A retainer is payment in advance for services to be rendered. It is rather like a down payment, showing your good faith in the lawyer's expected performance, just as the lawyer is showing his/her good faith in your future payment in full. If the lawyer insists on a retainer, you should ask if it will be refundable if the case ends up consuming less time than initially believed. You should also understand whether hourly fees are charged against the retainer, so that you will pay no further fees until the retainer is used up, or whether the lawyer will bill you regularly, keeping the retainer as insurance against future payment default.

Get It in Writing

Once you decide on a lawyer you want to handle your case and you have agreed with the lawyer on a fee, you should record your understanding of all the arrangements in a letter or agreement signed by both parties. This letter should include a fee payment schedule, and you might try to include a provision requiring your written permission before fees can run over a certain amount. In lieu of that, you could specify a maximum number of hours not to be exceeded. Two copies of the letter should be signed, and you and the lawyer should each retain one signed copy. You should not proceed without such an agreement until you have dealt with a lawyer for a long time and are confident of his/her billing procedures, integrity, and honesty. And even then, for complicated matters, we recommend a written understanding of representation.

Either you or the lawyer can originate the letter. However, before you sign, make sure that you understand each and every word in the agreement and that you have no doubts about any of it. Now is the time to ask any questions you may have—don't be hesitant or shy.

Detailed Bills

During your interview, you should ask how bills will be itemized. The more detailed your lawyer's bill, the less likely the chance of error, and the greater your understanding of exactly what work has been performed in your behalf.

If you are paying on an hourly basis, a bill that simply states an amount "for professional services rendered" is not acceptable. During the interview, ask to see a sample of the lawyer's bill to another client, with the client's name deleted. See if the bill is detailed as to time spent and the nature of each item, including the names of persons to whom telephone calls have been made, and the purpose of each call. Expenses should be detailed as to the type, reason, and exact cost (receipts should be supplied whenever possible).

Court Costs

If you actually go to court over a problem, make sure that you understand how the costs of the litigation, known as "court costs," will be paid. In most cases, these costs are repaid to the winning party by the losing party after the verdict. Court costs, sometimes called "record" costs, vary from state to state and even within a given state. They can include docket fees such as those for filing the complaint; witness, investigator, court-appointed expert, interpreter, court clerk, and marshal fees; and fees for printing necessary documents and transcripts.

Prepaid Legal Plans

Many groups, such as labor unions or employers, offer prepaid legal plans that resemble medical insurance plans. In some plans, the group member pays a set fee monthly or quarterly and, for that fee, is entitled to either a certain number of hours or certain types of legal assistance. In another type of plan, there is no prepaid fee, but the plan gives you the right to consult with a lawyer for a reduced fee. Most plans encourage preventive law, to cure problems before they get out of hand. Before joining any prepaid plan, you should understand the cost and the coverage, and then decide if your own possible legal problems are such as to make the plan a reasonable investment for you. Remember that membership in such a plan could give you considerable peace of mind in addition to any specific dollar savings.

18

WHAT IF I CAN'T AFFORD AN ATTORNEY?

Hiring a lawyer can be costly, but someone without the financial resources to hire a private attorney should not despair.

First, you have the option of taking your claim to small claims court (see Chapter 10) if it is the type of claim that the court is permitted to handle. Second, you can try to bring your opponent into a low-cost arbitration or mediation procedure where an attorney is not required, and where the losing party may be required to pay all costs. And finally, you can try publicly paid attorneys; these include the Public Defender, Legal Aid, and other volunteer lawyer groups.

Public Defender

If you have been accused of a crime and cannot afford to hire a private attorney, you may be eligible to be defended by the Public Defender (known as the Voluntary Defender in some areas). The Public Defender is listed in the telephone book, or you can obtain the phone number at the courthouse or, usually, from the police department.

Public Defenders are government-paid attorneys who specialize in criminal defense. Because they specialize, they are usually skilled in the courtroom, familiar with court procedure and personnel, and up-to-date on the criminal law. In short, a Public Defender can be a good choice for criminal defense.

In addition, since all the work of the Defender's office is criminal, the attorneys tend to develop specializations within the criminal law, and you might find yourself defended by someone with much expertise in your precise problem.

Court-Appointed Attorneys

In lieu of the Public Defender, or in areas where no Public Defender exists or where the type of offense is outside of their jurisdiction, the court may appoint a private attorney to represent an accused criminal who cannot afford to retain a lawyer in his/her defense. Court-appointed attorneys are paid by the government.

Legal Aid

While the Public Defenders handle *criminal* matters, Legal Aid offices deal with *civil* problems. Most cities have a Legal Aid (also known as Legal Services or Community Legal Services) office to service individuals who have a civil problem and cannot afford a private attorney to act on their behalf. As with the Public Defender, the Legal Services offices are funded by the federal government, although there has been some recent Congressional activity to eliminate or reduce the program.

Economic guidelines exist to determine if you qualify for Legal Aid. In addition, many offices limit their practice to certain types of cases. In one major city, for example, the types of cases handled by Community Legal Services include divorce, dependency and support hearings, landlord-tenant problems, liens, foreclosures, sheriff's sales, credit problems, debt collection, bankruptcy, unemployment and employment problems, immigration, consumer problems, veterans benefits, social security problems, medicaid and medicare problems, and welfare problems.

Volunteer Lawyer Organizations

Lawyers often volunteer their time and expertise to help people in their areas of specialization who may not qualify for Legal Aid but who still cannot afford a

80

specialized attorney. For example, lawyers often offer services to people in certain professions.

One such group is the Volunteer Lawyers for the Arts. This is an organization of lawyers who help artists, dancers, actors, musicians, etc. with personal and professional problems for a lower fee than they normally charge or, occasionally, for no fee at all.

You should check the Yellow Pages of your telephone directory or your local bar association for a list of voluntary lawyer groups in your area.

Reduced-Fee Programs

In addition, many bar associations offer reduced-fee programs for the disabled, elderly, or handicapped. If you fall into one of these categories, check with your local bar association to see if such assistance is available in your area.

PART V—HOW TO BE A GOOD CLIENT

19

HOW TO WORK WITH YOUR LAWYER

Now that you know more than you did about choosing a lawyer, let us give you some tips on how to get the most from your attorney—and for the lowest fee. Remember that if you are a good client, your lawyer will save time, and in most cases, you will receive a smaller bill. The Reasonable Lawyer works best with a Reasonable Client.

Honesty

The first rule when dealing with your lawyer is to be completely truthful, accurate, and honest. Or, to use the courtroom phrase, "tell the truth, the whole truth, and nothing but the truth." Withholding information, telling only part of the story, or failing to disclose embarrassing or damaging details to your attorney can interfere with your attorney doing the best job for you and can seriously damage your case.

Remember three things. First, your lawyer works for you; he/she is not your judge.

Second, if you fail to disclose some potentially damaging fact, and the fact later is brought out, your lawyer cannot possibly offer an adequate reply on a point about which he/she is ignorant and for which there has been no opportunity to prepare.

Third, your lawyer is bound by the rule of confidentiality not to disclose the content of your discussions (unless they fall within the narrow exceptions discussed in Chapter 11). You may speak to your lawyer with complete candor and openness.

Let Your Lawyer Guide You, But You Are the Boss

There are many times during the lawyer-client relationship when the lawyer has to be the one to decide how to proceed. However, you must make it clear at the beginning of your relationship that no settlements, litigation, or other pivotal matters are to be begun or concluded without your express consent, and then only after you understand all the details and ramifications of the move. This is especially important during settlement negotiations.

Keep in Contact

You should receive copies of all relevant documents and correspondence from your attorney. If you do not receive anything, tell the lawyer to send you copies of all documents. This will help keep you current on your case and will show you what your attorney is doing.

At the same time, don't become a pest. You need not telephone your lawyer on a daily or weekly basis, and you should remember that he/she will no doubt bill you for telephone calls. But, if something important comes up, or if there is a change in your situation, don't delay—inform your attorney immediately. If your attorney is in court or too busy to answer your call, ask his/her secretary to set a time for a telephone call, a sort of prearranged meeting by phone. That way, the time will be comfortable for both of you, and you will be able to talk without interruption.

Respect Your Lawyer's Advice

You have hired a lawyer to give you advice and information on matters in which he/she is experienced. When your lawyer gives you that advice—don't ignore it. If you are inclined to reject the advice, think twice, or perhaps three times. Occasionally there may be a good specific reason for rejecting a lawyer's advice. But if you find you don't have confidence in the lawyer's judgment, consider getting a new lawyer.

20

10 WAYS TO SAVE LEGAL FEES

Having explained how you can be a Reasonable Client, we now conclude by offering ten ways in which you can help keep those legal bills reasonable as well.

Be Prepared For Meetings

Do your homework before meeting with your attorney. Bring all documents with you. Write out a chronology of events and facts relevant to your case. It is far easier for your lawyer to read a brief summary and then to ask questions based on it, than for you to recount each detail verbally.

Maintain a File

Start a file regarding each legal matter you discuss with your attorney. Keep all correspondence, chronologies, and documents in the file. Take the file with you to all meetings with your attorney and/or the opposition.

Keep up to Date

If you read an item in a newspaper or magazine that you think is relevant to your case, cut it out and discuss it with your attorney at your next meeting. Better yet, make a photocopy of the item and send it to your attorney with a note explaining why you think it is important to the case.

Be on Time

Don't be late for an appointment with your attorney. His/her time is your money. If you have to cancel a scheduled appointment, do it as far in advance as possible.

Pay Promptly

When your lawyer submits a well-documented bill to you for services rendered, try to pay it promptly. Remember that the lawyer has already done the work and may not be comfortable about proceeding further until he/she is sure that compensation will be forthcoming.

Don't Withhold Information

Be frank and honest with your lawyer. Failing to reveal information, even if you are not sure of its relevance, may not only seriously damage your case but may also necessitate revisions or additional work that could have been avoided if you had been forthright at the beginning.

Don't Be a Pest

As we said earlier, communicate with your lawyer when it is necessary, but don't become a nuisance. Don't make your lawyer spend time on phone calls, letters, or meetings except when it is necessary and productive.

Express Yourself

Many clients are afraid to express their feelings and desires to their attorney. You must tell your lawyer what is most important to you so that he/she can act accordingly. For example, if you are contesting an estate and both money and sentimental items are at stake, tell your lawyer which of them means the most to you. If it is the sentimental items, the lawyer's tactics may be different than if you were to stress the money. The lawyer has no way of knowing unless you express yourself.

And if you don't like something that your lawyer has done—speak up. If he/she continues to behave in a way that displeases you, you may have to think of changing lawyers. But first, let the lawyer know how you feel.

Use Small Claims Court

If your case is one in which small claims court is a possibility, consider filing your claim there and avoid legal fees altogether.

Seek Legal Advice Early

The most effective way to avoid large legal fees is to seek the help of a lawyer early, before the situation gets out of hand. It is far better to have a lawyer review a minor matter for a small fee than to wait until the problem grows to major proportions requiring a costly legal effort.

21

CONCLUSION

Using a lawyer to help you with specific problems or for general advice can prove invaluable. A trusted lawyer can be your greatest ally and confidant. If you have doubts about when to use a lawyer, remember:

> *An ounce of prevention is worth a pound of cure. (Traditional)*

But if you have failed to take the ounce of prevention, don't despair—for, as Sir W. S. Gilbert so aptly said,

> *The subtleties of the legal mind are equal to the emergency.*

Iolanthe, Act II

BIOGRAPHY—PHYLLIS C. KAUFMAN

Phyllis C. Kaufman, the originator of the *No-Nonsense Guides*, is a Philadelphia attorney and theatrical producer. A graduate of Brandeis University, she was an editor of the law review at Temple University School of Law. She is listed in *Who's Who in American Law*, *Who's Who in American Women*, and *Foremost Women of the Twentieth Century*.

BIOGRAPHY—ARNOLD CORRIGAN

Arnold Corrigan, noted financial expert, is the author of *How Your IRA Can Make You A Millionaire* and a frequent guest on financial talk shows. A senior officer of a large New York investment advisory firm, he holds Bachelor's and Master's Degrees in economics from Harvard and has written for *Barron's* and other financial publications.